'92 To Barb From MariJo

IMAGES OF A SEASIDE RESORT
Cape May

IMAGES OF A SEASIDE RESORT
Cape May

Designed by Bernard Ben Pearce

PUBLISHED BY THE JARED COMPANY
WILMINGTON, DELAWARE

Copyright 1991 Mike Biggs and Tom Carroll
The Jared Company

All rights reserved. No part of this publication may be reproduced or transmitted in any form without the written permission of the Jared Company, Book Division.

THE JARED COMPANY
833 Locust Street
P.O. Box 1948
Wilmington, Delaware 19899

Published 1991
Printed in Hong Kong
Library of Congress Catalog Card Number 91-23630
ISBN: 0-89802-614-8
First Edition October 1991

PHOTOGRAPHER: Mike Biggs
TEXT: Tom Carroll
PUBLISHER: Maxim Dadone
DESIGN DIRECTOR: B. Ben Pearce
PRODUCTION: Michael Brugman
EDITING: Regan Goldstein and Sue Carroll

Cape May, Images of a Seaside Resort, has been made possible in part by the generous support of two major business leaders of Cape May County. First Southern State Bank, the county's newest full service commercial bank, and National Group of Cape May, representing National Associates, CNI and National Marine Insurance Companies have played an important part in the renaissance of the Cape May Community.

National Group and First Southern State Bank join together to salute the newest addition to the business and recreational community, the Cape May National Golf Club. One of the most naturally beautiful courses in the state has been carved out of the countryside and coastal environs to create the perfect blend of protected open space with appropriate recreational use.

Acknowledgements

I would like to thank the following people for their assistance with this book: Maxim Dadone, for his faith and support; Ben Pearce, for his creative input; Dottie Truman, for introducing me to Tom Carroll; and, of course, to community leader Tom Carroll and his lovely wife, Sue. Their love of Cape May was inspirational, and their generous hospitality was appreciated.

To the other community members that helped me along the way, I sincerely thank you.

WILLIAM G. GAFFNEY
Mayor

JOSEPH W. FOX
Council Member

ROBERT W. ELWELL, Sr.
Council Member

CITY OF CAPE MAY

National Historic Landmark
643 Washington Street
Cape May, New Jersey 08204-2397
(609) 884-9525

J. FRED COLDREN
City Manager

VIRGINIA E. PETERSEN
City Clerk

Cape May is the best preserved late 19th century seashore resort in America and a National Landmark. Its Victorian charm and culture as well as its natural beauty bring great pride to both visitors and residents alike. It is with great pleasure that I invite you to enjoy Cape May . . . Images of a Seaside Resort.

Wm. G. Gaffney
Mayor

Dedication

Though we were strangers until a year ago, Mike Biggs and I have shared an appreciation for the seashore most of our lives. We have both witnessed the effects of overdevelopment in the Mid-Atlantic region with the resulting destruction of historic communities and environmentally sensitive areas. Our appreciation for Cape May is only intensified by our awareness of the developmental pressures that face such a unique community.

We would like to dedicate our book to the residents of Cape May who have recognized the special beauty and the historic importance of their town and have worked so hard to protect those irreplaceable qualities. Their efforts will continue to safeguard this National Historic Landmark for the benefit of future generations.

TOM CARROLL

Preface

It didn't take long to fall in love with Cape May. My very first visit nearly ten years ago took care of that. Its Victorian architecture displayed in a multitude of colors was absolutely breathtaking — a photographer's dream. Add a touch of 19th century Victorian ambience and I was hooked.

When I finally managed to point my camera at something other than a Victorian home, I soon discovered the natural beauty of the area . . . parks, wetlands, and dunes surrounded by an ever changing ocean that demanded my attention.

I appreciate the efforts of Cape May residents like Tom and Sue Carroll who have fought to preserve this special community, and I hope that my photographs may, in some small way, serve to benefit their cause.

MIKE BIGGS

Introduction

Have you ever noticed the reaction when someone mentions Cape May? The very name brings forth instant recognition and inevitably a smile. It wasn't always that way; I can remember when people had never heard of my adopted hometown. That is not surprising when you consider that Cape May had nearly forgotten its own existence. After almost 60 years of sleep, Cape May awakened in the early 1960's, and to many residents' and visitors' delight, has succeeded in reclaiming its Victorian nickname, "The Queen of Seaside Resorts."

While rocking on the veranda on a lazy summer afternoon, Mike Biggs and I decided to explore the rebirth of Cape May in photographs and words. What were the factors that caused Cape May to save its architectural heritage, to fight to maintain its open spaces, and to develop the type of year around attractions that offer a true quality experience so untypical of a seashore resort community? While neighboring communities proceeded to add more fast food chains and pave over all vegetation, Cape May continues to take advantage of the best of the 20th century, while keeping a balance with its history and natural environment.

Cape May had shared a similar economic decline and revitalization with other historic communities. Nantucket, Massachusetts; Charleston, South Carolina; Saratoga Springs, New York; and Galveston, Texas, experienced decline and decay as industry, government or just the whims of vacationers moved in different directions. The decline of the whaling industry for Nantucket and the Civil War for Charleston had the same effect as the generational change of taste had on Cape May at the turn of the century. As one generation has typically rejected the taste and values of its parent generation, Cape May watched as the children of its aging clientele deserted the "Grand Dame" for the newer, more fashionable resorts. The towns that boomed in the early 20th century, like Atlantic City, Asbury Park, and Coney Island, have also witnessed the inevitable ups and downs of the tourist trade.

Economic decline has historically proven to be a valuable preservation tool in our country. The lack of reinvestment for half a century or more has protected many a historic district from unappreciative remodeling or demolition. It has bought time and allowed younger generations to discover a new quality of life available in homes and towns that have acquired a patina only time can create. For Cape May, the decline of the resort trade saved the greatest concentration of late 19th century structures in the country. As these gingerbread buildings changed hands in the 1970's and 80's, a new population arrived — people who found in Cape May a quality of life that so much of America has let slip away.

The natural barriers of ocean, bay and wetlands kept Cape May somewhat unto itself, a community not afraid of being different from other seashore resorts. Although it is no longer an island community, the open spaces that separate it from the mainland have always helped to protect it from commercial aggression while providing some of the most beautiful natural areas in New Jersey. Dilapidated historic structures that would not have survived in any other community have been restored to perfection. Ocean front spaces that could have been lined with condominiums now offer some of the best birding on the eastern seaboard. Music, theater, and many special events, along with cozy country inns and fine dining have created year around attractions.

Mike Biggs' photographs have successfully captured this new Cape May, its natural and manmade environment, its fun and serious side, its sunsets, seasons, gardens, verandas, and endless rolling surf. Working with Mike has brought back great memories of Cape May's progress: the purchase and restoration of the Physick Estate, the development of the Cape May Point State Park, the construction of the firehouse museum and the bandstand and even the first house that was painted a color other than white. These images remind us of many pleasurable moments we all have experienced — foggy mornings, the honking geese overhead, and the afternoon sun bathing the wetlands with a golden glow. They explain what is so difficult to put into words, the endless fascination that man has with the sea.

Mike and I hope this book will present not only the beauty of Cape May but the proud accomplishments of the many groups and individuals who have never turned their backs on a needy project or good cause. Never has there been a town with more people committed to protecting their quality of life. These beautiful photographs were truly made possible by all the people who cared so much to preserve their historic community and their precious natural environment.

*C*APE MAY *is a town of visual surprises. Every corner turned brings another architectural delight, and every beach walk provides endless varieties of cloud formations, sparkling waves, and a multitude of shore birds. The community was designated a National Historic Landmark in 1976 because of its great concentration of Victorian structures, and equally important, its independent, small town atmosphere.*

*C*APE MAY'S *gingerbread trim, or sawn ornamentation, represents one of the great folk arts of the 19th century. Carpenter builders took great pride in these original creative designs, and one rarely sees duplication of patterns. Towers, gables, and dormers offered great opportunity for individuality in cottage construction.*

*M*ANY *of Cape May's most famous homes are merely frame, vernacular structures with wonderful, festive facades. The combination of brackets, barge boards, spandrels, and balustrades fit together like a patchwork quilt, creating beauty through complexity. Most of the trim was cut on location by the builder; however, early mail-order companies provided pre-cut ornamentation that could "modernize" a pre-Victorian structure.*

*C*APE MAY'S most photographed home, The Pink House, was not always pink, nor was it built at its present location. The structure was almost lost in the 1960's before preservation was seen as progress. The house was saved when the local newspaper publisher purchased the house for one dollar and financed the relocation and restoration of this gingerbread masterpiece. Architectural historians refer to the building as an example of "total decoration" while visitors prefer to call it the wedding cake house. The style has become known as Carpenter Gothic, referring to the lavish display of wood ornamentation on a simple, frame cottage.

THE Mansard style roof of the Queen Victoria represents one of the most prolific of the numerous Victorian styles. After the fire of 1878 destroyed 30 acres in the heart of the city, builders favored this popular Parisian style. Considered one of the more practical styles from an impractical period, this distinctive roof line continues its popularity in the 20th century.

CAPE MAY retained its popularity with southerners up to the Civil War, and their architectural preferences remain to this day. The Italiante style was perfect for the seashore. Long, slender windows under shady verandas, high ceilings and cupolas for ventilation, provided natural cooling by ocean breezes. The Mainstay Inn was built in 1872 as Jackson's Clubhouse, a gentlemen's gambling club before gambling was declared illegal in New Jersey in 1898. The club house was closed and sold, but the building and furnishings remain much intact to this day.

THE Emlen Physick Estate was completed in 1879 and was described in the local paper as "... unlike any other Cape May cottage." This stick style structure, designed by the renowned Victorian architect, Frank Furness, has been painstakingly brought back to its original appearance by the Mid-Atlantic Center for the Arts. The Furness touch is evident in the over-sized brackets, "jerkinhead" dormers and huge "upside-down" chimneys. Much of the preservation funding was raised locally through special events, such as Victorian Week, which continue to benefit the entire community.

*F*ROM *Poverty Beach to Cape May Point, the graceful blend of old and new design continues to demonstrate the endless architectural possibilities of a seashore home. Although these homes are separated by over a hundred years, they still share the common elements of oversized windows, multi-leveled porches and colors of nature so sympathetic to their setting in the dunes.*

WHILE many of the architectural styles of the Victorian age were borrowed from abroad, the porch or veranda was truly an American adaptation and was an absolute must for the seashore. The invention of the automobile and resulting visual and noise pollution moved people from their front porches to their backyards throughout our country. This architectural feature almost disappeared from the American landscape. For Cape May, the popularity of the porch remained as strong as the attraction of the ocean itself.

ROCKING *is considered by some to be Cape May's most popular pastime. As one early visitor wrote in her diary, it provided "... a chance to see and be seen." This Victorian visitor's observation still accurately describes the experience.*

L AND was very expensive in Victorian Cape May. Homes were big and lots were small, but gardening was still popular. Victorian gardens, like the architecture of the period, rejected the formality of the Colonial period. The irregularity of the landscaping was considered to be more in harmony with nature.

*U*NLIKE *the typical sand bar communities of the Mid-Atlantic coast, Cape May is the end of the mainland and could be fittingly described as the beginning of the Garden State. Moist ocean air and fertile soil create gardens spilling over with impatiens, hydrangeas, and lilies.*

ADVERTISEMENTS commending the natural health cures of ocean bathing have been found in Philadelphia newspapers prior to the American Revolution. Entire southern families came north to escape the heat and health hazards of the deep south and to enjoy the season in "Cool Cape May, twenty miles at sea."

The early popularity of this resort was based on the availability of water borne transportation. Sailing packets and later steam ships plied the Delaware bay during the summer season, transporting visitors from Philadelphia to Steamboat Landing at Cape May Point. The one day cruise compared very favorably to the two day horse and carriage trip over the rough roads of South Jersey. A beach front horse drawn trolley was built to transport visitors the two miles from the landing to Cape Island, as the town was first known. By the advent of rail transportation, Cape May was already an established premier resort.

***S**PRING at the shore has a way of teasing the outdoorsman. Warm, sunny weather comes in the morning and just as quickly turns to a chilling ocean wind in the afternoon. With the approach of summer, cool ocean air collides with warm mainland breezes creating that mystical seashore condition — fog. The adversary of the navigator and the house painter is the delightful companion of the beachcomber.*

*A*s the ocean is warmed by the Gulf Stream, the fog disappears, and the beach is readied for the onslaught of summer crowds. The sound of the surf is soon to be accompanied by the laughter of families on vacation.

BEFORE the words "stress" became a buzz word, the sea offered the perfect, natural cure for that condition. Watching the endless waves rolling up the beach then retreating from a flock of hungry sandpipers, can relax the most jaded visitor. Through its own magnificence, the sea makes all problems minor by comparison.

F_{ALL} comes late along the coast. Warm ocean currents buffer the flow of arctic air masses and make September and October the favorite months for seashore natives. The migrations of monarch butterflies hint at the approach of fall long before changes in climate or colors of vegetation.

WINTER brings a quiet beauty to the shore. A walk along the beach provides privacy for thoughts and reflections and the crisp, clear air creates cloud formations and sunsets rarely experienced in the summer season.

THE *winter sun hangs low in the southern horizon, casting a golden glow upon the phragmites surrounding the ponds of the Cape May Point State Park. These pristine areas, accessible only by nature trails, display the natural transition from ocean and sand dunes to wetlands and mainland.*

*S*URROUNDED *by ocean and bay and the natural beauty of the State Park, the community of Cape May Point maintains a quiet winter vigil over the entrance to the Delaware bay. Lake Lilly, a fresh water pond, was discovered by the British fleet during the American Revolution. Local legend indicates that the residents dug a ditch to allow salt water intrusion, preventing the enemy from using it as a water supply.*

CAPE MAY Point was the southern most tip of New Jersey until ocean erosion claimed much of the southeast portion and the City of Cape May acquired that distinction. The absence of commercial activity makes the community especially idyllic.

*M*OST *of the sandy islands of the Jersey shore were kept safe from man's desecration for years by the wetlands. These areas, once regarded as merely an obstacle to transportation, are now protected by law as we have grown to appreciate their importance in coastal ecosystems. The wetlands are among our most valuable natural resources, having a significant effect on water quality and fisheries, and providing habitat for many forms of wildlife.*

F*OUNDED in 1976, the Cape May Bird Observatory has been conducting research on the migrations of hawks and owls through Cape May. More than 60,000 of these seasonal visitors have been banded in an effort to track their origins and destinations. The hawk banding demonstrations in September and October provide birding enthusiasts with a close inspection of a great variety of raptors on their journey south. Hawk counts are conducted annually to monitor fluctuations in population; over 50,000 hawks are spotted each year.*

THE Cape May County Peninsula acts as a natural funnel for millions of birds on their southern migration. As the land ends and ten miles of ocean lie ahead, the Point becomes a natural foraging and resting site for the birds. Rest stops vary with species, ranging from a few hours, weeks, or the entire winter. The fall migrations prove the most spectacular with song birds, waterfowl, shore birds, birds of prey, and sea birds gathering for the transit across the Delaware Bay. In the spring, northbound shorebirds arrive on the beaches of the Delaware Bay and feed frantically on horseshoe crab eggs. For many, it will be the only stop on their flight to the Arctic tundra.

*S*OME *people consider gulls to be a nuisance, but there is nothing lovelier than their graceful flight at sunset.*

E*ARLY visitors to Cape May resided in boarding houses seasonally operated by local farmers, fishermen and bay pilots. By the middle of the 19th century, however, the town's economy and character clearly reflected the resort nature of the community. The beach front developed an architectural richness as festive and varied as the summer activities.*

THE eccentric design of the Dr. Hunt cottage presents a deliberate contrast to the formal styles of the urban environment. It is a seashore vacation home that reflects a holiday spirit. Mixtures of Gothic, Mansard and Italianate details create a facade that exhibits a unique form of Victorian competition, decorating the decorations.

*T*HE *majority of visitors sought accommodations in the hotels that lined the beach front. By the 1850's, about 50 grand structures like the Congress Hall Hotel offered excellent dining, spacious rooms, and private baths, occasionally with hot and cold salt and fresh water. The restoration of the remaining grand dames of this Victorian resort represents one of the greatest challenges to this preservation minded community.*

***R**ELIGION played an important role in the life of the resort. Cape May Point was founded as Sea Grove, a religious retreat, in 1875. Unlike its more playful neighbor Cape May, Sea Grove prohibited the sale of intoxicating spirits. The wonderful chapel, Saint Peters by the Sea, enjoyed prominence at the Centennial Celebration in Philadelphia before being moved to Cape May Point. Its simple varnished wood interior contrasts with the magnificence of Our Lady Star of the Sea in Cape May proper.*

*T*HE Cape May Lighthouse has withstood many a furious storm and has witnessed innumerable glorious sunsets. Thanks to the efforts of local preservationists, it will continue to guard our coast indefinitely.

THROUGHOUT our history, from early Indian tribes through the stuffy Victorian period, every generation has found enjoyment in the sun, sand and surf. However, bathing habits have certainly changed. The Victorians believed that a tanned complexion identified one with the working classes; therefore, they chose to enjoy the ocean in the early morning and late afternoon. Since few individuals could swim, the gradual slope of Cape May's beach and its gentle surf added to the resort's popularity.

CAPE MAY holds a valid claim to the title, The Nation's Oldest Seashore Resort; however, most of the beach front was not developed until the second half of the 19th century. Earlier builders favored construction at a safer distance from the ocean. The beach was hard and wide, and carriage rides along the surf led to automobile races in the early 20th century. Henry Ford's unsuccessful racing career in town caused him to abandon his idea of manufacturing automobiles on a family farm at what is now the southern end of the Garden State Parkway.

*T*HE *normal gentle swells of the Atlantic Ocean can change to majestic proportions with the passage of an offshore storm or a Nor'easter. While rip tides cause beach closings and disappointed bathers, surfers will appear at any season of the year to make the best of the thundering surf.*

W*HILE the ocean and beach will always hold the attention of summer visitors, Cape May's other attractions provide enjoyment throughout the year. Nothing can quite compare to a horse and carriage ride. A turn around town in a gaily decorated carriage for some is the most memorable part of a wedding.*

*F*INDING *new uses for old buildings is one of the greatest challenges for the preservationist. The Cape Island Antiques once served as the stables for the residential area of Cape May. The bakery is one of many Washington Street Mall structures that has benefited from the pedestrian favored redesign of the town center.*

*T*HE open air Washington Mall was financed through the Urban Renewal Program, and it is considered to be one of the country's most successful renewal projects. The goal from the beginning was to preserve as many Victorian structures as possible while altering the roadways to encourage visitors to explore the historic district on foot. There is no better way to see Cape May than on one of the many popular walking tours of the historic district.

CAPE MAY'S cottages were built by the wealthy upper classes of the 19th century. Besides grand porches and parlors, they contained numerous bedrooms for family and friends, and still more for domestics. These summer mansions became white elephants in the 20th century real estate market until the advent of the bed and breakfast industry. Cape May today rightfully enjoys the title, "The B&B Capital of America." The town's innkeepers have led the country in this creative adaptive use of historic structures.

ANTIQUES once hauled away from Cape May for sale or auction in a more appreciative market are now returning. The town's numerous inns offer a delightful balance between historic decor and 20th century comforts. Good conversations and afternoon tea on breezy verandas have become the preferred vacation style for many of Cape May's new visitors.

THE Garden Room of the Washington Inn is only one of many fine dining spots which abound in Cape May. Sidewalk cafes, back street verandas, and a dock side schooner provide ideal settings for a variety of pleasant dining experiences.

SINCE 1823, the perilous shoals off of Cape May Point have been guarded by a lighthouse. This magnificent present day sentinel has swept its beacon 19 miles to sea continuously since 1859. Modern navigational equipment reduced the mariners' dependency on lighthouses, and the proud structure began to show the resulting neglect. In an effort to combine maritime history with interest in the Victorian era, the Mid-Atlantic Center for the Arts leased the lighthouse from the Coast Guard and began an extensive restoration.

SINCE the Cape May Lighthouse was opened to the public in 1987, an average of 60,000 visitors each year have climbed this architectural masterpiece to enjoy the view from the lantern room gallery. From 150 feet up, the panoramic view encompasses Cape May, the bay and ocean, and on a clear day, the Delaware coastline. One can't help but to reflect on the relief this flashing light provided to weary sailors as they approached landfall, the most dangerous portion of their ocean crossing.

*S*UDDEN *changes of weather are not peculiar along the shore. They become more frequent and violent as summer turns to fall. Silvery clouds race down the Delaware Bay bringing a damp chill and sending all but the most ardent beachcomber in search of shelter. The beauty of a new season is upon us.*

*T*HE *winter beach offers many surprises. The wind can whip the sand and sea spray through the air one minute and be as gentle as a summer day the next. Ocean water temperatures protect the area from sub-freezing weather making snow on the beach a rare but beautiful experience.*

W*INTER brings another dimension to the beauty of Cape May. Victorian England introduced the tradition of decorating for Christmas, and Victorian Cape May keeps the fine tradition very much alive. Houses, shops, and restaurants come alive with lights and greens inside and out and welcome visitors to enjoy the Christmas season in a setting right out of Dickens.*

VICTORIAN homes were made for Christmas. The ornate oak stairs, landing, and stained glass window of the Manor House offer endless opportunities for decorations. Many home owners have researched Victorian decorating traditions and combine humor and history during the popular Christmas Candlelight tours.

*V*ICTORIAN *Week was first introduced as a fund raising event for the restoration of the Emlen Physick Estate. This October week features Victorian fashion shows, dance workshops, house restoration demonstrations, concerts, plays, antique forums, and of course the ever popular house tours. The Victorian gala at the Christian Admiral Hotel is one of the social highlights of the season.*

THE Emlen Physick Estate had become a vacant haunted house by the 1960's. Its imminent demolition so upset the community that a preservation reform movement won the majority of seats on city council and accepted State and Federal assistance for purchase and restoration funds. Today, the restored 18-room mansion provides a fine example of an 1880's Victorian interior. Trained docents present an excellent interpretation of lifestyles and social customs in the 19th century.

*A*s the appreciation for Victoriana grew in the 1970's, every organization attempted to make its contribution. The Cape May City Volunteer Fire Department was looking for a location to display its proud possession, a 1928 American La France fire engine. A small lot adjacent to the Fire House presented the perfect opportunity to replicate a Victorian Fire Station, complete with tower for drying hoses and wall space to commemorate the great fires in Cape May and the dedication of generations of volunteers.

*A*s summer arrives, boats of every kind appear in the Cape May Harbor, picturesque sailboats along with powerful yachts. Many well known off shore racing skippers developed their competitive spirit at an early age sailing in the Cape May Harbor.

FOR many, the motion of a rocker and a view of the activity on the ocean offers sufficient nautical experience.

*C*APE MAY *is the fourth largest commercial fishing port on the East Coast based on the market value of its catch. The fishing industry is second only to the tourism industry in the Cape May area. Scallops, surf clams, flounder, mackerel, squid and lobsters are processed in the Cold Spring Harbor before heading to markets throughout the Mid-Atlantic region. If you enjoy clam chowder from a can anywhere in the country, it's a good chance it came from Cape May.*

THE whaling industry supported the first permanent white settlement in Cape May County. Today's modern fishing equipment stands in sharp contrast to the shore launched whale boats, but many of the dangers still exist. The Fishermen's Memorial which stands guard over the Cape May Harbor depicts a fisherman's family in quiet vigil, awaiting the safe return of those who venture out to sea.

*C*APE MAY, situated at the confluence of the Atlantic Ocean and Delaware Bay, provides a perfect home port for the United States Coast Guard. The northeast end of the community has served the Army, Navy, and most recently the Coast Guard since the American Revolution. Navy seaplanes, blimps, British frigates, German U-Boats, and Coast Guard rum-runner interceptors have all seen action and death off the beach of Cape May.

EVERY "Coastie" remembers Cape May in a bitter sweet way. Boot camp provides eight weeks of intensive training, turning carefree young men and women into sailors in the nation's oldest seagoing service. Every Friday, graduation brings tears and cheers as new found friends depart for assignments along every coat and waterway in the United States.

*T*HE *haunting motto, "You have to go out, but you don't have to come back," expressed the respect for the sea and dedication to service of the volunteer members of the US Lifesaving Service. This forerunner of today's Coast Guard began on the Jersey Coast in response to great losses at sea as winter nor'easters pounded sailing vessels, often overloaded with immigrants, and drove them helplessly into the breakers.*

MAN'S desire to reside by the ocean puts him in constant conflict with nature. The sandy barriers that separate the wetlands from the ocean build and erode in an unpredictable pattern. Any interface with dunes and natural vegetation inevitably exacerbates the erosion process.

A TTEMPTS to alter the movement of sand along the coast have only slowed, but never stopped, the process. The location of both the 1823 and 1847 Cape May Lighthouses are now long lost to the sea.

THE area affectionately known as "the cove" to every beach hiker was once the community of South Cape May. Homes and hotels lined the beach, and the trolley from Steamboat Landing passed by a favorite attraction, The Light of Asia, one of four huge wooden elephants constructed on the East Coast. The area is now owned by the State Park Service and the Nature Conservancy and will remain as dedicated open space.

BETWEEN the turn of the century and the 1960's, Cape May experienced very little resort-related construction. As the town's renaissance was just beginning, many investors turned their backs on our Victorian heritage and sought to construct a new, modern Cape May. With the appearance of several, oversized edifices, the community recoiled and created a master plan and zoning ordinance that would encourage and favor preservation projects. The response was not immediate, but eventually structures such as the Angel by the Sea were saved by zoning that downgraded the value of the land and favored historic buildings.

EVEN the most staunch defender of Old Cape May can be cynical at times. Will Cape May be consumed by its own success? Will its new popularity destroy the very quality of life that attracted the preservationists in the 70's and 80's? Change will inevitably occur; however, growth can be properly controlled and directed if citizens and city leaders work together to that end.

THE political consensus of the community is clearly for tightly controlled growth. City ordinances restrict development of open spaces, require set backs and buffer zones, and define the architectural flavor of the community. Air and water quality considerations remain uppermost in the minds of the city's environmentally aware population.

THE residents of Cape May are among its greatest assets. Many of them chose to live in Cape May because they appreciated its unique character and its special beauty, and they will work hard to retain these qualities.

C*APE MAY lies so close to urban America, yet in spirit, so far away. It will continue to provide its appreciative audience the pace and many pleasures of 19th century America.*

About the photographer...

Mike Biggs has sold his photographs as wall decor and stock photos for over fifteen years. His work has been used exclusively in seven calendars as well as three coffee table books.

A graduate of the University of Delaware, Biggs is a counselor at the Stanton Campus of Delaware Technical and Community College and resides in Bear, Delaware.

About the author...

Tom Carroll came to Cape May with the Coast Guard in 1969. Along with his wife, Sue, they opened the Mainstay Inn in 1971, combining their interest in preservation and the hospitality industry. The Inn, a former 19th century gentlemen's club, enjoys a national reputation and was one of the first bed and breakfast conversions in the country. Tom served as Chairman of the City Planning Board and assisted with the development of a master plan and zoning code that promoted preservation efforts in the community. As a former President of the Mid-Atlantic Center, he encouraged the organization to undertake the restoration of the Cape May Lighthouse. He now represents the southern region of the State of New Jersey Historic Trust.

About the designer...

Benard Ben Pearce is an award winning graphic designer employed at Stanton/Wilmington Campus of Delaware Technical and Community College. Dynamic Graphics of Illinois; the Government of Trinidad Postage Stamp Commission; and Delaware's IABC are among those who have honored him. He has designed and illustrated several books. Pearce holds the Bachelor of Fine Arts degree in graphic design and illustration from the Columbus College of Art & Design in Ohio and an M.A. degree in graphic design from the University of Baltimore in Maryland.

Calendar of Events

January - February

Presidents Weekend Craft and Antique Shows
Cape May Cooks, inn sponsored cooking school

March - April

Easter Weekend Egg Hunt and Stroll
Edgar Allan Poe Mystery Weekend
Tulip Festival

May - June

Audubon Society Weekend
Crafts at Memorial Day
Great Cape May Foot Race
Cape May Music Festival
Victorian Fair
Grand Lighthouse Ferry Cruise
Period Porches and Parlors Old House Tour

July - August

Cape May Summer Theatre Festival
Vintage Film Festival
Cape May Kids' Playhouse
Independence Day Celebration
Art League Membership Outdoor Art Show
Art Kane Photography Workshop
Sand Sculpture Contest
English Tea Party and Fashion Show at the Physick Estate
Art League Photography Show

September - October

Cape May Bird Observatory Hawk Banding
Washington Mall Art Show
Cape May Artist Studio Tour
Victorian Week

November

Sherlock Holmes Weekend
Crafts in November
Bed & Breakfast Seminar for Prospective Innkeepers

December

Dickens Christmas Extravaganza
Christmas Candlelight House Tour
Inns at Christmas Time House Tours
Annual Christmas Lights Competition